PRAISE FOR *REPURPOSED*

"You'd be silly to start a building project without a blueprint. But it's even crazier to approach retirement without a plan. Repurposed offers the kind of practical ideas that can transform your golden years into something absolutely priceless."

Dave Ramsey
Best-Selling Author and Nationally Syndicated Radio Show Host

"Do you want to live a life of significance through your retirement years? Ben Taatjes is a living example of servant leadership and he has written his book with the same wisdom, dedication, and respect that guides his life. In Repurposed: The Untold Story of Retirement in America, Ben shares the secret to a fulfilling retirement is to get clear on your purpose and how you will serve others during the greatest years of your life. Living the principles of this book will ensure you leave a legacy that will positively impact future generations."

Mark Deterding
Author and Founder of Triune Leadership Services

"An easy-to-read and down-to-earth message, Taatjes helps us all find purpose in our later years—and that is a most worthy endeavor!"

John G. Miller
Author of "QBQ! The Questions Behind the Question"

"We hear a lot about retirement being that magical time when we can move into a season of life of leisure, doing only what we enjoy doing. And yet reality shows us it's often simply a time of being "too old to work but too young to die." Without a clear plan, that time can be frightening and full of struggle. Repurposed is a guide for planning the last years of life, based not just on having enough money, but on continuing meaningful relationships, memories and legacy."

Dan Miller
Author and Coach (48Days.com)

"Ben's ability to think outside the box in his retirement planning and business is a tremendous benefit to his clients. I have seen this benefit firsthand both personally and with the clients I have referred to him over the years."

Ron Grussing
Retired CPA and Partner, Grussing, Bonnema, & Wrede, CPAs, PLLP

"After working with Ben and his team recently, I was able to successfully unwind my farm operation of more than 50 years in a tax efficient manner. And that was just icing on the cake. The true benefit in working with him was the ability to address the uncertainty from changing from a farmer to a retired farmer, which wasn't an easy task."

Ron Manthey
Client and Friend

"From the first time working with Ben several years ago he showed a genuine interest in me as person and my own retirement goals. I feel as if I'm part of a family with the team at Taatjes Financial Group."

Dave Danielson
Client and Friend

" 'Repurposed...' is a practical and honest journey to capture the heart of what it means to fully emulate a life well-lived from start to finish. Ben's focus on the whole person living each day with vigor and purpose inspires the reader to thoughtfully engage, especially the latter years of life, with renewed energy and passion. Retirement should not accidently happen. Retirement should be fully embraced with a passion to make a difference in our world. This book will help lead the charge into what could be some of the best years of your life!"

Pastor Steven Zwart
Senior Pastor, Unity Christian Reformed Church

BEN TAATJES

REPURPOSED

BEN TAATJES

REPURPOSED

The Untold Story of
RETIREMENT IN AMERICA

Throne Publishing Group
2329 N Career Ave #215
Sioux Falls, SD 57107
ThronePG.com

DEDICATION

To my wife, Megan, for her love, encouragement, and support in my work. Her example of selflessness as she moved from teacher, to mom and volunteer leader inspires me daily.

To my daughters, Lauren and Addilyn, who keep me grounded and make me smile every day with their love for me.

To my parents, whose teaching and modeling of stewardship has impacted my life greatly.

To my Grandpa Ervin, for his inspiration in giving and whose quiet lesson on stewardship now has a larger platform to impact God's Kingdom.

To my clients, who have shown me firsthand the joy and fulfillment found in living a life of impact long after their working years.

To my Savior Jesus Christ, who has given me life and the ability to work and create.

TABLE OF CONTENTS

PART ONE: EXPECTATIONS

1. A Dirt Bike Perspective of Money   3
2. The Showroom   13
3. Retirement as Marriage   27
4. Guaranteed Unhappiness   39

PART TWO: PREPARATIONS

5. The Worst Retirement Advice I've Ever Given   51
6. Preparing Well   61

PART THREE: LIVING

7. Practicing Retirement   75
8. Money Doesn't Buy Happiness, but Pensions Do   87
9. Legacy   97

Conclusion   *107*
About The Author   *113*

PART ONE

EXPECTATIONS

CHAPTER ONE

A DIRT BIKE PERSPECTIVE
OF MONEY

Popular culture portrays retirement as a continual vacation filled with nothing but comfort and carefree living. What it doesn't show, however, is its mental, emotional, spiritual, and physical toll. As with many things in our world, reality isn't always as advertised. My goal is to help reframe and reset those expectations of retirement. Rather than a comfortable cruise to the end of life, retirement can be a spring season of renewed purpose and fresh satisfaction. In the following chapters, I want to help you prepare well for a retirement marked by two things: fulfillment and well-deserved rest.

I want to help you prepare well for a retirement marked by two things: fulfillment and well-deserved rest.

One of the biggest revelations of my career was when I realized living out my life's purpose is the only way to true fulfillment. This path is walked by contributing to the lives of others. I discovered this through work with a trusted friend and mentor, Mark Deterding, author of *Leading Jesus' Way.* Mark was leading me through some material pioneered by his own mentor, Ken Blanchard, that was intended to connect people with their greater life purpose.

At this point, Mark and Ken challenged me to think deeper than I ever had before while creating a personal purpose statement and trace back to a specific event that shaped who I am today. And then it came to me, the story of how my first dirt bike impacted the way I view money. If you've never done this, consider finding some time to do it yourself because, for me, it was powerful. Through this process, I uncovered that my real purpose wasn't something like, "I want to continue to grow my business." Instead, it was to positively impact as many lives as possible. From this single story of a hand-me-down, relic of a dirt bike, the way I run my business changed forever. To begin, I'd like to share this story that helped me clarify my past, present, and future on this earth.

THE DIRT BIKE

My third-grade school year had just wound to a close, and it was my first summer of freedom on the tattered seat of a 1975 125CC Yamaha Enduro dirt bike. To the outsider, this bike looked like it belonged in a dusty barn rather than the open field, but to me, it was absolutely beautiful. From the dinged-up gas tank to the broken headlight, it held a rugged character forged by years on dirt roads and pastureland, and growing up on a farm, I was surrounded by a circle of adventure miles wide.

The bike was given to me by my uncle, who then showed me the secret to starting it. First, you had to get a running start and jog alongside it. Once you were rolling, you could hop into the saddle and feel the engine croak to life beneath you. I first learned to ride around our farm then progressed to gravel roads and dirt trails, but my favorite place to ride was the gravel pit, a twenty-mile ride from home. My older brother and two of our friends had motorcycles as well, so that summer we lived on those things—after our morning chores were finished, that is.

My parents raised hogs, and we had two farrowing barns; one was my responsibility and the other my older brother's. First thing each day, we scooped manure and then hurried off to our dirt bikes. For little boys beneath wide-open skies, it was like riding through heaven. However, after a couple of summers on this bike, something shifted in me. One of my friends got a dirt bike as well, only his didn't have the fresh-from-the-creek-bottom look that mine had. His bike was newer than mine and had smooth paint, slick decals, and working lights. He rode around on a seat without rips and tears, and did I ever want the dirt bike like he had! So after a summer of comparative glances at my friend's bike, I begged my dad to take me into town for a new dirt bike.

To this day, I still don't know how I convinced him, but he finally took me to the showroom of Motor Sports of Willmar in Willmar, Minnesota. When we stepped foot into the showroom, we were greeted by the smell of tires and fresh plastic, just like that new car smell, only better because these machines were designed for nothing but fun. I couldn't have been happier, because there she was, gleaming beneath the lights: the Honda XR 100CC. It had no broken lights, no scratches, flawless paint, a perfect seat, and an abundance of shiny decals. At that moment, it was everything I had ever dreamed of. The problem was, this motorcycle had a hefty price tag of $1,500, which was about $1,000 north of my liquidity at the time. Miraculously, though, my dad stood in the gap and allowed me to trade in my perfectly working Enduro and take a loan from him to cover the rest. The deal was that I had two summers to pay it off. I quickly accepted and signed my name to his dotted line.

My initial elation slowly evaporated on the drive home, however, and flatlined when we pulled into our driveway. My first case of buyer's remorse had set in, replacing the contentment I had enjoyed atop my weathered Enduro. In fact, on my new XR's maiden voyage, I crashed into an old stump in our yard, hidden beneath the tall grass. So suddenly, my pristine dirt bike wasn't perfect anymore; it had received its first black eye. To sour the deal even further, because I had purchased the bike in the fall, winter soon set in, which in Minnesota means I wasn't going to ride the bike for months. So it waited quietly in storage for the following summer. But rather than days filled with riding, the next summer brought days filled with hoeing beets. After all, I had to pay off the loan to my father.

Every morning, I woke up early, performed the chores still expected of me, and then rode my XR to my day job at a nearby farm. If you're not familiar with hoeing beets, it is tough work. Your days consist of walking endless rows beneath the hot summer sun, chopping weeds, and uprooting the occasional sugar beet planted too close to its neighbor. Then, once my day of toiling in the field was done, I drove my bike home, did my evening chores, and collapsed, only to wake up the next morning and do it all over again.

THE DEBTOR

As I reflected back on this story while crafting my personal purpose statement, it dawned on me that all of my favorite memories were of careening down the trails on my trusty, old Enduro, whereas my new bike, the XR, brought only memories of maintaining and washing it along with a daily commute. The simple fact was that this bike owned me; I didn't own it. So over the two summers that I worked hard to pay it off, I learned what it was to be a debtor. And in an ironic ending, when I had paid the loan off and the title was officially mine, I was too big for the bike and sold it to my younger brother for 500 bucks.

In this, I learned firsthand this ancient, New Testament truth: "Yet true godliness with contentment is itself great wealth. After all, we brought nothing with us when we came into the world, and we can't take anything with us when we leave it. So if we have enough food and clothing, let us be content" (1 Timothy 6:6-8 [NLT]). The lesson imprinted on me was that I had exchanged the contentment in the experiences I enjoyed on the Enduro for the expectation that the new dirt bike would make me happy in and of itself.

But this is life, isn't it? How many times do we invest much of our focus and effort for a house that's bigger or a car that's newer than we need? Everything we look at every day is based on the goal of most advertisers: making us feel that everything we have is not good enough. This cycle never ends, but we still line up for it every time.

After creating my purpose statement and reconnecting with the financial lesson of my first dirt bike, I realized that I was made *to glorify God daily by leading others to a life of contentment and financial peace.* I had expected that dirt bike to make me happy, but I was let down because it couldn't deliver on the happiness I thought it held. Just as it was true for a fifth-grade boy, it's true for adults of all ages: our purpose on this earth is far greater than the accumulation of things. Instead, true wealth is found in our legacy's positive impact on people's lives. This is the vantage point from which we will examine planning for retirement in the pages that follow. Having worked with hundreds of clients in the past decade, I have learned that just like my experience in the showroom of Motor Sports of Willmar, retirement isn't exactly what it's presented to be. However, with the right mindset, it can be more fulfilling than you ever thought possible.

CHAPTER TWO

THE SHOWROOM

It's no secret that every day we are swarmed with ad campaigns designed to make us crave what's next and covet what's not ours. One of the primary stages on which this plays out is in achieving financial success. However, the problem with this kind of success as a motivator is that it's a moving target. Its definition is always changing. While I'm not advocating for mediocrity or neglecting excellence, I do want to make one thing clear: by default, we cannot find fulfillment in a moving target because it is constantly redefined. This puts us on a path where our craving can never be fully satisfied, and thus we cannot be truly fulfilled. This is the very definition of false hope, just as I found out after leaving the showroom.

In today's society, this attitude of consumerism is the anti-contentment message, and it has invaded our view of retirement. In this chapter, we will uncover that the description on the label is not really what's in the package by tracing retirement to its origins and unveiling the emperor with no clothes who stands behind it all. To begin, let's consider some timeless wisdom from the best-selling book in history.

In today's society, this attitude of consumerism is the anti-contentment message, and it has invaded our view of retirement.

THE BLOWING WIND AND EVER-FLOWING STREAMS

Millennia ago, wise King Solomon wrote: "The wind blows to the south and goes around to the north; around and around goes the wind, and on its circuits the wind returns. All streams run to the sea, but the sea is not full; to the place where the streams flow, there they flow again. All things are full of weariness; a man cannot utter it; the eye is not satisfied with seeing, nor the ear filled with hearing" (Ecclesiastes 1:6-8). Consumerism sets us on a path of chasing the wind because right when we think we've arrived, fulfillment slips from our grasp, compelling us to chase it all over again. Worse yet, it's been true for thousands of years that our eyes are never satisfied and will always hunger for more. This is our plight, and it shows up in every part of our lives. Now, if we fast-forward to the Apostle Paul's first letter to the Corinthians, he chimes in on the same premise. He described a world that is "passing away," and just like the winds that blow and streams that flow, the things in our world are fleeting shadows.

Regardless of whether you are a Christian, deep truths are found in these verses, and throughout the rest of the book we will visit Bible passages that illuminate the points and principles we're discussing. These two passages in particular ring like church bells, don't they? They precisely describe how most of our world functions.

When I reflect on my first dirt bike, I realize that it was in a very literal sense simply a vehicle that I found happiness through. My hand-me-down bike didn't have to make me happy in and of itself. Instead, it was a machine that I owned, rather than something that owned me. The second bike, though, was exactly the opposite. It made me a debtor and controlled how I had to live my life. In the end, it was fruitless to place my hope there. The writer of Lamentations speaks to this well, saying, "'The LORD is my portion,' says my soul, 'therefore I will hope in him.' The LORD is good to those who wait for him, to the soul who seeks him. It is good that one should wait quietly for the salvation of the LORD" (Lamentations 3:24-26). As leaders, Christ followers, and everyone in between, whatever we place our hope must be able to deliver on its promise, and this will never be true of things.

Another of Paul's letters reads, "As for the rich in this present age, charge them not to be haughty, nor to set their hopes on the uncertainty of riches, but on God, who richly provides us with everything to enjoy" (1 Timothy 6:17). God provides dirt bikes for our enjoyment, rather than as ends in and of themselves. The same is true of financial gain and even the season of retirement.

Now, whether or not you are a person of faith, take a moment to reflect on your life. Where have you placed your hope in the things that sparkle in the showroom of life, and when have any of those things ever fulfilled you? I would wager that they never have, as they haven't for me either. Recently, my eleven-year-old daughter, Lauren, learned this lesson too.

SEVEN, SEVEN, CUCUMBER

She came to me crying, upset that an American Girl doll in her room had gotten destroyed. I responded, saying, "Lauren, I have not one thing from my room when I was eleven. What I have are memories, not things." Does this ring true? How many things do you still have from even a decade ago? Probably not many because they are continually replaced by something newer and better. There's always more around the bend.

There is nowhere that I see this phenomenon play out more blatantly, however, than in my work in retirement planning. Retirement is elevated as the oasis found in the desert of our working years. For our entire careers, it is the thing that we scrimp and save for, and the sole purpose of our 401Ks and IRAs. However, just like the showroom of life, it's a rigged system if we don't see beyond the veneer. In fact, it's eerily similar to how slot machines in casinos are designed to work.

While I'm not a gambler, I do know there is a reason the casino is bigger than your house and mine: it always wins. Imagine people standing in front of slot machines. They insert their quarters and then pull the levers. With jackpots on their minds, they watch the three dials spin. Numbers and shapes whir in a blur of possibility. Then the first wheel stops: *seven*. Then the second wheel stops: *seven*. Their mouths gape open and they lean forward, thinking, *I could actually win this!* Then the final dial snaps to a halt—only, instead of seeing another seven, they're greeted by the lumpy, green shape of a cucumber.

They came so close to winning; for an instant they could taste it, and they realized that the quarters might magically transform into hundreds of dollars. So what do they do? They spin again. After all, it's only a few quarters, right? Of course, this is how the house always wins. The slot machines are fixed so that people are always *almost* winning. They get so close, only to have their chances dashed at the last second. In turn, this perpetuates the cycle of trying again and again: insert a coin, pull the lever, be disappointed, and repeat. This is precisely the way many of our lives look today: a blur of numbers and shapes with that elusive jackpot just beyond our fingertips. Now, if wealth, material possessions, and retirement are the proverbial slot machines in the showroom of life, where did it all begin, and was it intended to be this way?

THE GENESIS OF RETIREMENT

I don't pretend to be a historian, so you're going to read a layperson's perspective. However, the genesis of retirement is fascinating and far removed from how we view it today as an endless vacation. Wind the clock back hundreds of years, and you will find that the average person's life expectancy was much shorter than ours today. In 1889, German Chancellor Otto von Bismarck engineered a revolutionary social concept to appease the growing tide of Marxism and socialism: old-age pensions. Based on Bismarck's idea, German Emperor William I wrote: "Those who are disabled from work by age and invalidity have a well-grounded claim to care from the state." The idea was that those who were "disabled from work by age" or who had reached the age of seventy could retire and receive the financial security and benefit of a safety net. Retirement was first intended for people who could not feasibly provide for themselves, more for necessity than for rest and relaxation, and seventy was a full twenty-five years beyond the average life span.[1]

Nearly forty years later, on August 14, 1935, Franklin D. Roosevelt signed the New Deal, or the Social Security Act, into law. This guaranteed an income for the unemployed and retirees. Thus, the age of sixty-five for retirement was codified into America's social structure as the age working years were over. Initially, as Roosevelt said, the goal was to "Give some measure of protection to the average citizen and to his family against the loss of a job and against poverty-ridden old age."[2] This rationale was similar to Bismarck's, but came with the benefit of luring older workers from the workforce to make room for younger, unemployed workers. Early on, retirees were not overly excited about the idea of being "too

1. "The End of Retirement," *The Economist*, June 25, 2009, accessed October 26, 2016, http://www.economist.com/node/13900145.
2. "Franklin Roosevelt's Statement on Signing the Social Security Act." Franklin D. Roosevelt Presidential Library and Museum. Accessed January 24, 2017. http://docs.fdrlibrary.marist.edu/odssast.html.

old to work but too young to die" and in fact dreaded this signal of nearing the end of their useful lives. Ernest Burgess of the University of Chicago was a significant contributor to the notion of retirement in the 1940s and 1950s and described retirees as being stuck in "roleless roles."[3] As decades progressed, the financial services industry, the new idea of pensions, and a few newly minted retirement communities transformed retirement from an end-of-life signal to one of leisure and permanent vacation. In 1950, nearly half of men over sixty-five remained in the workforce, but by 2000, less than 18 percent were still working.[4]

Since the end of the nineteenth century, it's clear that both the form and function of retirement changed dramatically. Perhaps the greatest fuel for this change was the advent of the Social Security system because as our societal understanding and approach to retirement shifted, this made way for an entirely new industry to emerge: retirement planning. Today, however, the age of sixty-five is the new forty-five. So even though our life expectancies have skyrocketed, the age of retirement has remained static, becoming largely arbitrary.

---

3. Marc Freedman, *Encore: Finding Work That Matters in the Second Half of Life* (New York, NY: Public Affairs, 2008), 43.
4. Ibid., 37.

RESPECT AND THE SILVER CROWN

From this structure, a cultural belief system has developed and shifted our conception of retirement. Today, younger generations, by and large, view retirees and those of old age as less relevant and having a poor ability to significantly contribute. Yet in my experience, this couldn't be further from the truth. In fact, one of the reasons I love what I do so much is that people who are approaching retirement have more to offer in almost every facet of life than just about anyone else. They have rich life experience, financial stability, and time to invest. On the whole, these three assets alone should set them up as prime players in our world.

If we rewind a couple of millennia, we see this reality well established in the Roman Senate. In fact, the word *senate* is derived from the Latin *senex*, which means "aged." In Roman society, you wouldn't have seen thirty-somethings in positions of governmental authority. Instead, the leaders were world-wise, older men who had gained substantial wisdom through years of life experience. This meant that reaching old age wasn't focused first on rest and relaxation, but rather on service to and leadership within the community. Older age was meant to produce a legacy that would perpetuate itself from generation to generation, which is why one of Solomon's proverbs declares that silver hair is "a crown of glory" gained in "a righteous life" (Proverbs 16:31).

Our thinking regarding both retirement and old age has departed from this significantly. Rather than viewing retirees as people with treasure troves of value to add, we see them as people past their prime. This notion is fostered by everything from commercials to magazines, where retired couples are shown driving RVs, smiling happily, and making comfort their continual goal. Now, in no way is rest after a life spent earning, working, and adding value to society a bad thing; it's a very good thing. But retirement isn't just a finish line; instead it can be the beginning of the greatest leg of the race. Your retirement years can be your most fulfilling when you pursue them for the right reasons.

But retirement isn't just a finish line; instead it can be the beginning of the greatest leg of the race.

Consider this: the global population of retirees is projected to double to nearly 1.3 billion by 2040.[5] The sheer volume of people entering this age bracket will dramatically alter the world's future—for better or worse—but think about the massive opportunity for good through investing in younger

5. "OECD Statistics," accessed November 22, 2016, https://stats.oecd.org/.

generations, generosity, and a legacy mindset. The potential for positive impact is staggering. In the coming decades, retirees have an unprecedented opportunity to shape the world for the better.

SPRING IS COMING

I've witnessed this hold true in a variety of ways, but one of the most profound has been through the life of retired US Navy Admiral Bruce Clingan. He retired in his prime as one of the highest-ranking naval officers in the world, serving as Commander of US Naval Forces Europe, US Naval Forces Africa, and Allied Joint Force Command Naples. Thousands of men and women were under his authority, and he led well.

He stepped down after thirty-seven years in what are often considered the autumn years of life. In this season, the leaves have turned to hues of orange, yellow, and red and are closer each day to falling to the ground. However, what Admiral Clingan modeled is that just because leaves are destined to fall to the ground doesn't mean the tree is no longer alive. When he retired, he took what could be thought of as a winter's rest, but then the springtime came, and he became intensely involved in Youth for Christ USA, an organization that spans the nation in its reach and impact.

Through this ministry, fresh leaves have blossomed in a new season of life. Just as trees grow green in springtime, Admiral Clingan's life is flourishing and nourishing those under his care. Trees produce fruit and provide shade; they exist for the benefit of those around them. In providing us with fruit and shade, they wonderfully fulfill their purpose.

This is a beautiful picture of retirement because it is a season that can be filled with life-giving rest for the retiree and life-providing fruit for others. When people live in accordance with a purpose greater than themselves, fulfillment is made possible. That is why I love my clients; they are stepping into what can be the most rewarding, fulfilling, and influential years of their lives all because they embrace the idea that they were made for a purpose greater than just having a comfortable rest at the end of their lives.

CHAPTER THREE

RETIREMENT AS MARRIAGE

D o you remember your wedding day? You were dressed in a tuxedo or stunning white gown, ready for decades of happiness, right? That's how I felt on my wedding day. I couldn't wait for years of bliss with a beautiful new roommate who always smelled nice. I had grown tired of rooming with guys, so how could this new life not be perfect? Now, however, having been married to my wife for sixteen years, I know that while we are perfect for each other, it's not in the way I expected. Just like marriage, retirement isn't what people expect it to be.

It's easy to anticipate days of endless relaxation and contentment, but often the picture retirees have differs substantially from reality. This isn't to say retirement can't be an incredible season, because it certainly can. In working with many clients, though, I have discovered that the key is setting the right expectations. So whether people are either soon-to-be newlyweds or retirees, a clear picture of what's really in store is a crucial component of happiness. While I'm certainly not a marriage expert, this will be a helpful analogy for us as we look deeper at retirement.

RETIREMENT AS MARRIAGE

From my vantage point, the most selfish way to pick a spouse is to look for someone who will complete you. When this is the case, marriage becomes an exercise in using someone else for your fulfillment. It becomes another showroom where our lives primarily unfold for our enjoyment, where we are ushered into a dazzling fantasy, tailor-made just for us. Mercifully, this is not how my marriage began.

My wife and I were married in a small town. We held our ceremony at the church she had attended growing up, followed by a simple reception. Our fancy dinner was ham-and-cheese croissants, and our entertainment was an emcee who said a few simple lines. Our focus wasn't on the wedding day; it was on getting married. That's what made us excited. Today, though, weddings get bigger by the year, and so do their budgets. Just like the retirement business, there are mountains of money to be made when the focus is placed squarely on the dreamy façade packaged neatly in marketing campaigns. In fact, the romantic imaginings of "the big day" often begin when girls are small.

We have two young daughters, and people constantly tell us, "You better start saving for their weddings right now!" To which I reply, "It's OK; inflation isn't too bad on ham-and-cheese croissants." Obviously, we know that for my girls to have happy, healthy marriages, the emphasis cannot be on the wedding day. It needs to be on the life that unfolds because a great ceremony doesn't equate to a great marriage.

THE MARRIAGE MINDSET

As my girls grow up, I hope to instill in them the right marriage mindset, and I will encourage them to get solid premarital counseling. This will help wash away the naïve veneer of a flawless marriage, because—as we who have been married for any amount of time know—that's impossible. There are problems when even one human is involved in something, much less two. If they approach marriage with false expectations, they're set up for disappointment before they begin. They will make mistakes, and so will their spouses, and this is OK.

Interestingly, I'm not the only one who thinks proper expectations are important for newlyweds. I live in Minnesota, and here, if engaged couples submit proof of premarital counseling that includes conflict management skills, their marriage license fee is reduced by over 50 percent. The state does this because, in the long run, it will save significant money in legal proceedings because these marriages tend to outlast those that don't begin with such counseling. When proper expectations are set, couples have the opportunity to peer into reality, rather than have their fantasy world dashed upon the rocks of life.

NO ROOM FOR AUTOPILOT

An important facet of setting the right expectations is taking care to watch for bumps along the way. My friend Bruce has an incredible Lear jet with a two-pilot cockpit. Recently, I got to sit in the copilot's chair. As we were in the air, he warned, "Ben, don't touch anything. I took it off autopilot earlier than normal." I put my hands in my lap and watched him keep alert, making manual adjustments and carefully checking his instruments. You see, we were on the right course when we took off, but should the unexpected arise, he couldn't abandon the controls. Flying, just like marriage and retirement, is not a set-it-and-forget-it affair.

Flying, just like marriage and retirement, is not a set-it-and-forget-it affair.

No one approaches either of these life-altering events with a desire to be disappointed. To ensure my clients are never caught off guard, I act as a preretirement counselor. Retirees step into massive life changes, so when unexpected challenges surface, I want them to be ready. Our culture paints a picture of retirement in every commercial that stars couples zooming around the country in an RV, sporting content smiles. They enjoy the relaxation they've been waiting their entire lives for. However, just like a little girl's lifelong dreams of the perfect wedding day, our expectations of a carefree retirement aren't what they seem. If you retire for the wrong reasons, your decision will ultimately disappoint you.

SETTING EXPECTATIONS

The first myth to dispel is that retirement will bring an end to stress. You have been working hard, running a business or raising a family for years, so stress-free living is attractive. However, what will you do with the eight hours or more per day you used to spend working? How will you fill that time? Will you be spending that time with your spouse or pursuing the hobbies you've always placed on the back burner? This is a more substantial adjustment than it seems, and just like marriage, this new stage in life brings unexpected difficulties.

The reality is that if you haven't learned to deal with stress before retirement, you still won't know how after retirement, and retiring won't make it disappear.

Next, retirement is not the epitome of fulfillment. Recently, a friend of mine retired. She had been looking forward to it for years, like many of us do. However, she realized that it wasn't what she expected. It wasn't as restful as she had anticipated, and she wasn't fulfilled like she was while working. So she went back to work. Incredibly, she's not alone. We've seen many clients do the same because they didn't find what they thought they would on the other side of sixty-five.

It's likely that you, just like my friend, are not being "called" to retire. In essence, our purpose on this earth is not to work hard so we can eventually stop and live out our days sipping from drinks with little umbrellas in them. While rest is certainly part of a fulfilling life, it is not the sum of it. So when people retire without planning and realistic expectations, lack of purpose and calling is an acute issue. For example, recently I consulted with a woman who had been retired for five days. I asked her how she liked it and what was on her agenda that day. She replied, "Well, I have two things to take care of today: I need to check my mousetraps and rake my leaves."

To many of us, that sounds like a wonderful day—less the mousetraps—but consider this: just a week prior she had worked as a nurse. She was alleviating pain and helping people heal; she had a defined role and was making an incredible contribution to society. Now, she didn't fail in her retirement or leave my office listless and miserable. However, it is important to note what a stark contrast and radical transition retirement can be. In the span of one week, she went from patient care to mousetrap duty. Can this new season be serene and restful? Absolutely. But if you are unprepared, it can also result in feelings of unfulfillment and purposelessness.

SETUP FOR SUCCESS: BILL'S STORY

What I have experienced and what we see in our clients' lives is that I am happiest and healthiest when giving to and serving others. This is true for my marriage, my relationship with my daughters, my church, and every other relationship I have. Retirement is the same way; to be fulfilled, we must have a purpose beyond ourselves. Self-focus will never result in the highest quality of life. This was proven to me most decidedly by one client's retirement.

> **What I have experienced and what we see in our clients' lives is that I am happiest and healthiest when giving to and serving others.**

Bill was a gruff Minnesota farmer, toughened from years in the field and driving the combine. We were using high-end planning techniques to save on taxes and help him transition well financially. He had farmed for over forty years, had millions of dollars in equipment, and owned ample land. However, his children were not interested in farming. One day, he and his wife came in for an appointment, and I began with a simple question: "Bill, we've run all of the numbers, and things look really good, but how are you going to leave the farm mentally?"

His wife looked at me and replied, "Not so well. I guess we need to talk about that more."

Our firm has a retirement coach on staff, but Bill didn't seem the type who would be interested. Given the circumstances, though, I offered: "Would you ever come in and talk to our retirement coach about how to prepare for that?"

Bill said, "I guess it couldn't hurt to visit."

I was shocked at his interest and imagined that he'd come in for fifteen minutes to half an hour. However, he was with our coach for over two hours on the first meeting and has returned for several more. Since then, his wife has hugged me and said, "Thank you for what you've done for Bill. He's a completely different man."

In the long run, I believe this will become standard practice for retirement planning because mental and emotional preparedness are just as vital to a happy retirement as money. I hope to play a role in leading this. It was true for Bill, and it's true for us all. Just like premarital counseling for healthy marriages, preretirement coaching is critical to happiness after leaving the workplace. It is a drastic life change, so if we are unprepared for reality, fulfillment will be difficult to find. As we will discuss in the next chapter, there are few guarantees in life, but one thing I can promise is that a "me-focused" retirement will be an unhappy one.

CHAPTER FOUR

● ● ◗ ◗ ◦

GUARANTEED UNHAPPINESS

In our business as retirement professionals, we can guarantee almost nothing because past results don't always predict future success. However, there is one promise I can make with confidence: if you make retirement about only yourself, you will be unhappy. This doesn't mean that you need to spend the rest of your life starting orphanages and clothing the poor, but what you do need to understand is that if every day is spent in orbit around yourself, contentment will evaporate.

What I have seen to be true is that the key is to focus on putting others first. This can range from the simple to the sensational. From putting your spouse's needs before your own to going on mission trips with your church, every day should have an element of service to other people. For example, I know of retirees whose goal in retirement is to golf every day. While this is OK, and they certainly deserve enjoyment and rest, will this lead to a fulfilling life?

Imagine you are a tree. You began, just as every other tree, as a sapling. Over the years you developed and grew; you were watered by the rain and fed by the sun. Eventually, your branches spread wide enough to provide shade and bear fruit for the people who surrounded you. This is the picture of a fulfilling life, a tree fulfilling its purpose. Retirement does not have to be the autumn of life. Instead, it can be the springtime, a brand-new season of flourishing, feeding others, and fruitfulness in daily life. In over a decade of work, I have seen this proven true time and again.

> **Retirement does not have to be the autumn of life. Instead, it can be the springtime, a brand-new season.**

SELFISH OR SIGNIFICANT?

For our entire working lives, we are value creators. If we spent a career in construction, we built things with our hands that we could see, feel, and touch. We can return and say, "I helped build that building." Our teachers spend decades pouring themselves into our kids. Line workers in manufacturing facilities make things that we use every single day. Our CEOs lead entire companies and impact hundreds of households as they do. However, when we retire without a plan to continue adding value, we are setting ourselves up to fail.

In retirement, failure equals unhappiness. Leadership expert John Maxwell challenges his grandkids to add value to someone else every day. What I love about this is that it cuts to the heart of what it is to be human; we were created to add value. However, when we live fully focused on ourselves and our needs, we will find a surprising emptiness. After all, Scripture tells us that we were created and made to serve. So if we see retirement as only a means to ending work, we miss an incredible opportunity to be happier and more fulfilled than we ever have before because selfishness and significance cannot coexist.

FLIPPING THE SWITCH

One of the most profound things Jesus ever said was, "It is better to give than to receive." Now, you don't need to be a Christian to experience the truth of this statement. Generosity is something we are wired to participate in. In Mark 10:45, we read that Jesus didn't come to be served, but rather came to serve, and in John 13, we see Jesus washing His disciples' feet and teaching them that no servant is greater than His master. This means that His followers needed to follow His example and serve those around them, and whether or not you follow Christ, living this way will certainly result in greater fulfillment.

Connecting to a cause greater than yourself paves the way to true happiness. Psychologist Martin Seligman discovered that there are three paths, or levels, to happiness. Imagine a pyramid divided into three horizontal sections. On the bottom is pleasure, in the middle is engagement, and at the top is purpose. So let's say you are a baseball fanatic. Using this pyramid, the quickest path to happiness is pleasure. In this case, attending the World Series would be incredible. Even greater happiness, though, would be found in engagement. This is moving from passive consumption to active participation or playing baseball instead of watching it. At the top, however, we find the most fulfillment in living out our purpose. For the baseball lover, the most fulfilling activity might be coaching baseball because it encompasses motivations beyond your own happiness and benefits other people.

This concept is also well illustrated by business expert Jim Collins. In a recent presentation, he talked about when his wife completed an Ironman competition. It is an incredibly grueling triathlon that only the world's most elite athletes ever finish. When she crossed the finish line, however, she felt a sudden emptiness. She had arrived at the moment she had trained so hard for, and now, in less than a day, it was over. But when she started training and coaching other athletes, Collins said it rocked her world. She became exponentially happier when she focused on helping others achieve their goals than in accomplishing her own.

Where are you in your retirement? Are you passively watching, are you engaged, or are you serving for a greater purpose? The deepest and most rewarding relationships are based on putting other persons' interests before your own. To live at the pinnacle of the happiness pyramid is to pass down your wisdom, knowledge, and experience. This is your legacy, teaching what you have gained and learned through a lifetime. When I taught my daughter how to shoot a rifle, the joy I experienced when I had first learned came exploding back. It was dramatically more fulfilling to see her shoot down a can than for me to do it myself. This is the beautiful part of flipping the switch. When we focus on benefiting others, we benefit ourselves just as much, and there is no season in life where this is more possible than in retirement.

There is no season in life where this is more possible than in retirement.

DIVINE DISCONTENTMENT

Ralph Waldo Emerson explored the idea of "divine discontentment," a state of knowing we are not really walking in God's perfect plan for our lives. In his book *48 Days to the Work You Love*, Dan Miller further describes Emerson's idea. He says this discontentment stems from a mismatch between "who we are and the work we are doing."[6] Miller writes that the cure is found in looking inwardly at your passion, recognizing where you have talent, and then finding economic validation for it. Economic validation means that there must be a market for your goods or services so you can get paid.

The beauty of viewing this process through a retirement lens is that you often need only two of the three; the income is generally less crucial because your finances are already in order. For example, maybe you have a strong musical ability and talent and a passion for leading praise and worship at church, but you couldn't create enough income to support your family. So you were never able to devote yourself fully to it. Retirement is a perfect time to give greater weight to your passions and abilities and less to financial considerations. In this season, to be happy and fulfilled, you need a forum to use your passion and talents in combination with a cause greater than yourself.

---

6. Dan Miller, *48 Days to the Work You Love* (Nashville, TN: B & H Pub. Group, 2010).

PURPOSE-DRIVEN RETIREMENT

To flip the switch for yourself, you must know what, for whom, and why you are doing what you do. This means that your daily decisions will flow directly from your life's purpose. Why do you get out of bed in the morning? The reason must be focused on either God or others. Are you retiring *from* something or *to* something? Why do you exist? Look back on your entire life. What things have you learned that you can pass on? Remember, selfishness and significance are like oil and water. They cannot combine to create happiness because they simply do not mix.

Are you retiring *from* something or *to* something?

PART TWO

PREPARATIONS

CHAPTER FIVE

THE WORST RETIREMENT ADVICE I'VE EVER GIVEN

As a retirement planner, I have learned that retirement must be approached holistically. It is more than spreadsheets and numbers because a happy life is greater than their sum. There is nowhere I have learned this profound lesson more than in the following story. As you've probably guessed from the chapter title, there is no worse retirement advice I have ever given than the advice I gave to a client named Jim.

Jim lived and worked his entire life in rural Minnesota. He spent a career working hard for a manufacturer. Over the years, he worked in various capacities, but most of it was manual labor. He did the heavy lifting, performing maintenance on sizable machinery, and ensuring everything on the factory floor was in peak operating condition. Jim wasn't a grudging worker either; he loved his job. In fact, I would go so far as to say work was worship to him. He was a man of strong faith who understood that doing quality work with joy is pleasing to the Lord.

When Jim first visited my office, he was sixty-two years old and simply gathering information. As I looked at his numbers, I saw he had built up a sizable nest egg in a 401(k). He was diligent in his savings over an entire career and was in an excellent financial position, so much so that I gave him the most surprising news of his life. I told him, "Jim, I have great news for you. If you want to, you can retire right now."

He replied, "You mean I don't have to wait until I'm sixty-five? Will I have enough money?"

"That's right. We've calculated for risks and inflation, and with your planned spending, you will have plenty of income to retire today," I said.

About a week later, Jim visited our office and was very excited. He said, "Guess what, Ben? I took your advice and put in my two-week notice."

"That's great," I said. "If you can retire now, you should."

With that, Jim said good-bye and left happy as can be. Now, you may be wondering why this was such bad advice. After all, the plan was financially sound, and he was certainly ready to retire—on paper, that is. However, as we

While Jim's bank account was ready for retirement, he wasn't.

explored in Chapter Four, there is a component of retirement that I had not considered. While Jim's bank account was ready for retirement, he wasn't.

THREE MONTHS LATER

Three months later, Jim and his wife came in for an appointment. She was still working, so he was spending a considerable amount of time alone. Even though only a few months had passed, he looked as if he had aged three years instead of three months. I could immediately tell something was wrong.

As we talked, I learned that all of Jim's friends were his former coworkers. So he was spending most of his time alone, watching television while his wife was at work. Besides a small amount of yard work and dabbling in some new hobbies, he was bored and had no plan. Additionally, because he had such a physical career, his new sedentary lifestyle was negatively affecting him. He was inactive, sleeping later, and moving visibly slower.

Mentally, he was already slower and seemed disengaged from life. He certainly wasn't the same upbeat man who had strutted into my office celebrating his retirement. He seemed like a man disconnected from his purpose because while he was working, he was adding value. After retiring, he completely

stopped doing that, and because most of his strong relation-
ships were with people from work, he rarely saw any friends.
After all, they still had to work every day, but he was at home.
This was hardly the picture the feasibility study forecasted for
Jim's retirement. The spreadsheets looked wonderful, but his
new life did not mirror the numbers.

EXPECTATIONS AND BLIND SPOTS

Looking back, I see that I was unknowingly marveling at Jim's
situation. The ability to retire three years early is incredible,
and I found myself wondering, "What could I do with that
time?" But I was seeing retirement in the showroom, viewing
it through the lens of cultural expectations, and so was Jim.
For him, a proper retirement plan was much more than numbers and risk mitigation.

Neither of us understood the real value and necessity of
community and purpose in retirement. When he took off his
work boots and left the factory floor, he left behind something far more valuable. He didn't simply leave a job for a
life of revitalizing rest; he left his community without having
anyone else to meaningfully connect to. I learned that one of
the most difficult challenges retired people face is isolation.
When you are surrounded by an empty room and television is

your only companion, life grows quickly bleak. Without realizing it, Jim had left his purpose at work and didn't have a new one to take its place. He didn't retire *to* a fresh purpose, but rather *from* his old one. In essence, it was like he had moved into an empty house that he expected to be furnished. Reality did not match the dream.

WHAT HAPPENED NEXT

When Jim left my office that day, I sat in silence thinking through what I had just seen. I had anticipated a man brimming with life, excited about his newfound freedom. Even though I had done my job, I had still failed this client. Retirement was supposed to make his life better, but it seemed to have taken it away.

Retirement was supposed to make his life better, but it seemed to have taken it away.

In our subsequent meetings, we discussed numbers for only a few minutes because they had a much smaller impact on his quality of life than either of us had thought. What I realized is that Jim hadn't initially come in to retire. He had been planning to retire at sixty-five, and those three years would have given him much more time to process and slowly say good-bye to his friends. A transition by degrees would have been much healthier and more helpful. I thought I was giving him his dream, but it wasn't what I thought it was.

Now, imagine that you walked into my office today and discovered you could retire tomorrow. What would you do? How would you live with purpose and significance and add value? Your life is more than a financial statement and more than a plan. That is what I learned firsthand from Jim.

From that point forward, I drew a line in the sand and became aware of the showroom of retirement. I understood that preparing well for retirement means far more than financial planning. Holistic readiness gives ample weight to the nonfinancial side of retirement. We crafted a new mission statement: "...to partner with individuals, families, and businesses to change lives and inspire 'True Wealth.'" Our focus shifted from growing assets under management to changing people's lives rather than only their wallets. The truth is, the nonfinancial risks can actually be greater than the financial ones. Simply put, if you don't address the nonfinancial issues, the financial ones will not matter.

Today, I seek to be effective by helping people plan for their lives, rather than just saving money. Rather than retirement planning alone, we are planning for life as well. I feel we do an excellent job of stewarding and managing clients' assets. However, they must have a purpose beyond the monthly financial statements, a greater reason for possessing them. We love to see clients use their funds in three ways: spend them in retirement, pass them on to the next generation, and donate them to charity. Having a plan and purpose to impact society is an integral part of our process today. Jim taught me that preparing well consists in far more than financial stability. That's why the plan beyond the numbers is our focal point, because that's where happiness and true wealth lie.

CHAPTER SIX

PREPARING WELL

Throughout our working years, we are bombarded with the idea that as long as we have enough money at the end of our career, we can retire happily. However, my experience with Jim showed me that my view of retirement was broken and our system of planning was flawed. Conventional wisdom failed, so it was time for a new way. That's when we began to approach retirement from a holistic perspective, and it begins with the definition of true wealth. My primary motivation is to help clients translate their financial assets into real life. By first determining what is truly important to them, we can set a plan in place to align their assets with the years to come.

When my clients leave our office, they aren't simply taking a product home with them. This is not a transactional business, because it is their life and legacy we are planning. What really happened is that I gained a fresh sense of responsibility, and my motivation to grow my business changed. It's a funny thing when you stop working for money and focus solely on helping people change their lives. My work is about growing

This is not a transactional business, because it is their life and legacy we are planning.

people, not just growing assets. Our business provides all we need, we have no debt, and we're moving forward, but not for the money, rather for a purpose.

Today, our retirement planning process flows from the simple lesson I learned from my first dirt bike: *contentment comes from neither money nor things.* The same holds true in business and retirement, and it is the principle that fuels me every day. My reason for existing is to help people lead a life of contentment and to glorify God. It is part of my DNA and infuses our company with meaning and passion. As my clients prepare for retirement, I help them consider their lives in five key areas: financial, social, emotional, physical, and legacy.

OUR PROCESS: FINANCIAL

When we first begin with a client, we start with retirement spending, taxation, inflation, risk management, and other important financial matters. While the nonfinancial aspects of retirement are crucially important, we do start with money because that is the foundation of preparedness. One of my favorite ways to do this is to ask my client this unexpected question: "How early do you show up to the airport?"

While the nonfinancial aspects of retirement are crucially important, we do start with money because that is the foundation of preparedness.

Now, here's why that is important. Are you the kind of person who shows up with only twenty minutes to spare, still expecting to make it through security and board your flight? I call these people underplanners because they habitually underestimate what they will need to accomplish their goals. However, there is a flip side. Instead of underplanning, do you overplan, showing up to the airport ten hours early? If this is the case, you've wasted eight hours of your day during which you could have done so much else. Our planning process helps our clients adequately plan for the income they will need without over-planning, which can lead to regrets later in life.

My ideal outcome is for you to show up at the proverbial airport with two hours to spare, not too late, not too early. That's the sweet spot where you live without regrets. After all, who wants to miss the plane or spend an entire day sitting in an airport terminal? Our goal is to craft the ideal plan that will sustain you through retirement while taking on the least amount of risk possible and where each asset has a specific goal tied to *your life*. Then, once the financial retirement plan has been developed and implemented, we monitor it and make necessary adjustments over regular meetings. This is where I used to stop, and most advisors still do. However, once we have the financial aspect of retirement accounted for, we now move into the nonfinancial factors.

OUR PROCESS: SOCIAL

I have a friend who told me that he felt as if he retired only to lose his entire family the next day because when he left, he left his close-knit community of work colleagues. If you recall, the most difficult thing for a retiree is isolation. After my friend retired, he couldn't simply walk back into the office, have a cup of coffee, and talk about how much free time he had on his hands. People who are still working have neither the time nor the inclination to brainstorm how to fill days of leisure for a new retiree. Social interaction also keeps people cognitively sharper than crossword puzzles or Sudoku. In-depth conversation will always win out over puzzles and trivialities.

One of the best examples of this is my grandmother, Oma. She lived into her mid-eighties and to the end was razor sharp. She was an engaged conversationalist, witty and clever, and an attentive listener. She raised twelve children, nine girls and three boys, so there was always plenty of family interaction. The standard notion in our family was that her habit of playing cards (a game called Schnozzle) is what kept her sharp, but I believe it was much deeper than that. After eighty years of playing this card game, mental gymnastics were no longer required. Instead, it was the constant social interaction and deep conversation with the people who mattered most to her that kept her sharp.

I am not alone in this theory. Noted author and psychologist Dr. Henry Cloud writes about this phenomenon in his book *The Power of the Other*. His brother-in-law was a Navy SEAL, and a key component in their training is a galvanized instinct to always ask themselves two questions upon landing in a combat zone: "Where am I, and where is my buddy?" Dr. Cloud explains that this is more than a simple operating procedure. It is actually a deeply rooted motivation to survive because they are not concerned with their personal fate alone; they are engaged with their fellow brothers in arms. This key factor harnesses the power of relationship, and Dr. Cloud describes it further: "We are talking about *specific qualitative relational connectedness*. Neuroscience has shown us that these kinds of relationships, even seemingly insignificant ones, greatly enhance performance and even help build, fuel, and sustain the physical connections hardwired in the brain."[7]

OUR PROCESS: EMOTIONAL

Attendant to the social components of our retirement planning process is emotional preparedness. One of the key facets here is the importance of others-focused themes. Not only does this facilitate social connection, but it also increases fulfillment significantly. While we do not force this, we do encourage it because of its consistently positive impact. Being emotionally and mentally focused on others aids in preventing isolation by facilitating meaningful connection. In fact, something I love working toward with clients is crafting a personal purpose statement. The takeaway here, though, is having something other than yourself to focus on and invest in.

Remember, as previously discussed, it's vital that you don't merely retire *from* work. Instead, retire *to* a new purpose—become *repurposed*. Fulfillment requires an investment in something bigger than yourself. It requires a life

---

7. Henry Cloud, *The Power of the Other: The Startling Effect Other People Have on You, from the Boardroom to the Bedroom and Beyond—And What to Do About It* (New York, NY: Harper Business, 2016).

lived for more than leisure because we were each designed with a purpose in mind. Contentment springs from a definitive understanding that you are fulfilling the reason for why you exist.

OUR PROCESS: PHYSICAL

Next, as I saw in Jim, physical health must also be taken into account. In the span of two weeks, he moved from a physically demanding job to a sedentary lifestyle, and when he visited our office again, it was obvious this cold-turkey transition had taken a toll on him. I won't belabor this point; there are plenty of good books on health, so I do not need to rewrite one here. Every one of us is simply happier, has more energy, and is more vibrant when our physical lives are in shape. This is why we counsel clients to stay engaged with their health to allow for more active and enjoyable retirement years.

OUR PROCESS: LEGACY

Finally, we address the capstone of a life well lived: *legacy*. Reflect on what's been important to you over the course of your life. Have you spent your time investing in it? Whether on people, organizations, or service projects, what value are you going to leave behind? At the end of your life, will you be able to look back with peace and contentment, knowing you served well? No matter how you answer these questions, the truth is that you can expand your legacy further in the coming season. Repurpose yourself in retirement and solidify a positive legacy. Leave behind a wake of purpose, value, and benefit, having lived the second half of your life as a life-giving source for others. This will result in true solace and joy because you will know that your corner of the world is better for your having lived in it.

FIRST STEPS

Every plan is only as good as its implementation. Even if we craft the most ironclad retirement plan in history, if it is not put into action, it won't do anyone any good. It consists of a series of questions broken down into both nonfinancial and financial aspects of retirement. Each question approaches these areas from a different angle and prompts our clients to think about retirement in new ways. There is a wide variety of questions, but I will share three of the most important with you here.

Every plan is only as good as its implementation.

1. **Social Connection:** Where will you find large-scale social connection?

   Consider where your closest relationships are currently. Are they at work with colleagues? At home with your family? In your church or other organization? Because social connection is critical, what is your plan to nourish those relationships and maintain them in this new season of life?

2. **Meaning:** Where can you move beyond pleasure and engagement to meaning?

   Recall Seligman's happiness paths, or levels, from Chapter Three. Where in your life can you move from pleasure and engagement—levels one and two—to happiness and meaning by investing in other people? To keep with our original example, where can you coach baseball rather than simply watch or play it? What is your plan to find purpose and add value to others?

3. **Legacy:** What can you do that will help people remember you as someone who added value?

   What legacy will you have to reflect on as you approach retirement and the end of your life? What impact on current and future generations are you going to have financially, relationally, and spiritually? What ripples do you hope to leave behind because you finished well?

In the final chapter, we will explore legacy at length; I know we each want to leave the world a better place for our having lived. It also provides us as retirement planners and coaches a deeper level of insight and a baseline to understand where you are now and where you'd like to be. So whether you are near to retirement or decades away, honestly wrestling with questions like these is a holistic gauge for retirement readiness.

Now that we have set proper expectations and touched on how to prepare, it's time to focus on living. Retirement can be the most fulfilling, enriching, and rewarding season of your life, a veritable springtime of happiness for both yourself and others. Let's turn to the practical, yet often overlooked, principle of practicing retirement.

PART THREE

LIVING

CHAPTER SEVEN

PRACTICING RETIREMENT

If you have spent any portion of your life playing sports or seriously pursuing a hobby, you understand well the old adage "practice makes perfect." Basketball players take thousands of shots to perfect their form. Golfers do the same with the mechanics of their swing. And where do surgeons begin? Do they step straight into the operating theater, or do they begin in a safe, controlled, and supervised environment?

The importance of practice is heavily ingrained in our understanding of what it takes to become a high performer in any discipline, personal or professional. But have you ever heard anyone talk about practicing retirement? Chances are, probably not. Why is this true when it is such a major life decision and transition? To begin, there are two professions that we will compare and contrast: teachers and CPAs. The first tend to retire well, whereas the second should but often don't. The reason why? Practice.

Let's consider career teachers who have taught for forty years and have reached retirement age. What practice do these teachers have that other professionals don't? They have a decades-long rhythm of mini-retirement each year. Every summer, if they don't teach summer classes, they disengage from work and have control over their calendar for three months. In doing so, they become what I call "talent chameleons" because they become very good at walking away from their job, trying new things, and fostering deep social connections. Even more, think of their legacy. Career teachers plant thousands of seeds in society, investing in and educating our children every single school year. They go to basketball games, attend high school graduation parties, and often counsel kids on their way to college and careers. All of this amounts to the satisfaction they feel knowing they played a part in their students' lives.

Now, what sets our teachers apart from CPAs? After all, CPAs work extremely hard all tax season, putting in long hours and working with hundreds of clients. Then they too take summers off for the most part. Like teachers, you would think they would have a rhythm of disengaging from work to rest as well, but the key differentiator is their facilitation of social connection. Many CPAs have deep and rich relationships with their clients because they grow so close to them through the tax-planning process. On paper, they should be just like our teachers in their ability to retire and enjoy quality relationships. However, what happens is that professional financial relationships are more difficult to maintain outside the bounds of the office.

While this isn't to say CPAs are doomed to retire poorly whereas teachers are destined for fulfillment, it is yet another broad case study for the importance of social connection beyond the workplace. So how can you practice retirement in your life and work?

WHAT IS PRACTICING RETIREMENT?

Practicing retirement is the proper mindset propelled by a plan. This means that prior to retirement, you really consider what your days are going to look like. What are you going to fill your time with? Where will you invest your time to find purpose? What truly gives you rest and rejuvenation? The reason for practicing retirement is because the first time we try things, just like free throws or golf swings, they usually don't go very well. Our first cakes come out of the oven flat, which isn't very fun when you are hosting a dinner party.

An easy place to start is by answering these questions: Can you leave your cell phone at home? Can you leave your work at the office? Do you have a life outside of work that you are excited to live? If the answer is no to any one of these questions, then consider this a gift to yourself. You haven't failed; you've been given an insight that will benefit you in the long run because now you have an opportunity to practice.

I have two clients who exemplify both extremes. The first client takes every January off, and when he's gone, he's really gone. He drops off the grid completely, disconnects, and is able to practice retirement. The second client, however, cannot even set his phone down. When he is supposed to be on vacation, he will call me to check on his portfolio because he doesn't know how to take downtime. Which one are you more like? Can you unplug and enjoy yourself? Or does that thought alone stress you out?

People don't talk about disconnecting from work; they don't think about it or even consider practicing it because our society does not reward those who rest. We idolize driving, going, and progressing at every moment of the day. We are constantly on the lookout for ways to increase our productivity and get more out of ourselves every moment. Again, we see ourselves and others on display in the

Our society does not reward those who rest.

showroom of business and life. In reality, many feel that if they take time off, they have done something wrong. For instance, how many times have you heard someone in the office mention an upcoming vacation, only to be met with statements like, "It sure must be nice to take a vacation; I wish I knew what that felt like"?

Disengaging from work is not something that should be frowned upon; it should be celebrated, especially as you approach retirement. If you are not the kind of person who can step away from work today, you will not magically become that person tomorrow. When you near the end of your working years, make certain you can leave work at work and let your life take shape outside of the office.

One of the best ways to do this is a method called "bridge work," or a transition into retirement. Bridge work is when employees in their early sixties begin a slow taper toward retirement. This allows an opportunity to progressively practice retiring and offers two other benefits. First, medical insurance or real income that is needed to prepare financially can be a great benefit in these last years of work. Second, the transition period allows for an unexpected phenomenon when you are planning for the nonfinancial aspects of retirement we have discussed in previous chapters. As you find new ways to add value and find purpose, you will notice that your job is getting in the way of pursuing new passions. This is the point where you can realize that the transition can be made to your benefit, rather than to your detriment.

We encourage clients in this position to try bridge work with their current employer or even to find a short-term career where it is an option. It is very healthy and often benefits both employer and employee. A recent study done by Encore.org of workers aged eighteen to sixty-four found more than 60 percent envisioned a gradual transition to retirement, and a greater majority of 72 percent planned to do meaningful charity work or work for extra income. I've seen these statistics hold true in our office as well.

HOW TO PRACTICE RETIREMENT

To begin, it's helpful to think about practicing retirement like going to the gym for the first time. Before you jump in and start lifting heavy weights, you need to establish a baseline. You need to understand where you are currently to define the path to growth. Could you leave the office for a month without getting cold chills? What about two weeks? Could you refrain from constantly checking and refreshing your e-mail outside of the office?

Let's take it from a different angle. Think about your last weekend off. How did it go? Did you really take time off, or was it interspersed with work? Are you able to be fully present in your role in your family or social groups? Can you engage as a mom, dad, grandpa, or grandma in the way you truly want to? You can learn a great deal about yourself when you ask these questions and answer honestly. Remember, just because it seems like you will have more time to get these things right when you retire does not mean you will.

Today, digging deeply into your strengths and weaknesses is easier than ever. There are many personality assessments and profiles available. Many are geared toward work, but the same rules apply across life. Find your passion and what makes you tick. Discern new ways to serve in these areas, and you will find yourself getting more and more excited to get out of bed every morning. Remove the economic pieces, and simply look at your talents and abilities. From there, you will enjoy a fresh vantage point to envision your future.

> **Find your passion and what makes you tick.**

MAKE A DAILY PLAN

I'm sure you have heard the analogy of the big rocks and pebbles. The concept is that we all have lives mixed with crucial priorities and less important tasks. The idea is that if your life is a bucket and you have large priorities, or big rocks, and smaller tasks, or pebbles, that all need to fit, you start with the big rocks first. That way, the most important things are accomplished, leaving room for the smaller things to fill the gaps between them. The same holds true for your retirement practice. What are those big rocks in your life, and are you making room for them right now? What are those things that will fulfill you and have you leaping up to greet the day? Make this prioritization a habit right now, and intentionally plan your day.

GUARD RAILS

Finally, there is a great importance in defining guard rails. What I mean is that whether we realize it or not, our employers have given us guard rails, or boundaries, to live and work within. They have defined everything from when we wake up, to when we eat, when we go home, and even when we go on vacation. However, when you walk away from the workplace, you also walk away from the structure that has been in place for so many years. There is something tremendously healthy about these guard rails, so to lose them completely is a danger.

Practicing retirement encompasses every aspect of your life, and the steps laid out in this chapter are an excellent place to start. Answer these questions, envision your future, and define the guard rails that are most helpful to you. What structures are most valuable in your personal and family life? How can you maintain them after you leave the workforce? Most important, do you genuinely have a life to look forward to outside of your job? Remember the example our teachers have given us, and habitually begin to disengage and practice rest. If you can do so, you will set yourself up to retire well.

There is still another important element to practicing retirement, however. You must shift your mindset not only concerning daily life, but also with money. Believe it or not, money is different once you retire, and understanding the distinction between wealth and income is paramount. For example, it's pleasant watching investment portfolios grow fatter by the year, but what happens when you need to start drawing from the wealth you've worked so hard to build up? What happens when the paychecks dry up and you are on your own? In the next chapter, we are going to tackle these questions and others head-on.

CHAPTER EIGHT

MONEY DOESN'T BUY HAPPINESS, BUT PENSIONS DO

From a very young age, my parents preached that money does not buy happiness. If you recall my dirt bike story, you'll know that we were not well off financially; we were a struggling farm family. I remember driving with my dad in his old truck and seeing people with fancy cars drive by. Without fail, he would say, "Ben, the smile on their face is no bigger than the smile on ours because money does not buy happiness." Even though I have made a similar case thus far, I have discovered an important nuance in the happiness equation.

In this chapter, you will survey the paradigm of wealth versus income and how each correlates to happiness. I believe you will find, just as I have, that the traditional view of wealth management can actually destroy happiness, whereas establishing a plan for retirement income makes it possible.

WEALTH DEFINED

What is the difference between wealth and income? At first blush, they sound similar, but the difference is both stark and important. I define wealth as an abundance of resources. It's a kind of stockpile that is continually filled up but rarely drawn on. Think of a grain bin that is filled year after year without having many withdrawals.

One of my favorite passages of scripture that illustrates the fault of wealth-centric thinking is Ecclesiastes 5:11: "As goods increase, so do those who consume them, and what benefit are they to the owner, except to feast his eyes on them." To me, that is what wealth can become. It is no good to simply watch the numbers on your investment statements grow and never use those funds. What does a stockpile of wealth do for you or provide to you if it simply sits in an account? Bill Gates, who knows a thing or two about wealth and income, said, "I can understand wanting to have one million dollars, but once you get beyond that, I have to tell you, it's the same hamburger." Simply put, after a certain point, what good is increasing your wealth?

INCOME DEFINED

Instead, what retirees need to focus on is income, which I define as money received on a regular basis to provide for your daily needs. Just like Jesus' prayer in Matthew 6, income is our "daily bread." It is wealth turned tangible and more a functional tool than a balance sheet. Income allows us to do things, whereas wealth is something to look at. Income is

Income is the useful side of money.

the useful side of money. It allows us to purchase goods and services and put food on our table.

You'll notice that this chapter is called "Money Doesn't Buy Happiness, But Pensions Do." I make that claim because income affords us the ability to buy experiences and do the things a meaningful life offers. When you can take a trip with your family that you have always dreamed of, you will remember it forever. Income allows us to do this for both ourselves and others. When we have a steady and reliable income, we can confidently give to charity and practice generosity.

DESTROYING HAPPINESS

To further illustrate this difference, here is a biblical truth found in 1 Timothy 6:17-19:

> As for the rich in this present age, charge them not to
> be haughty, nor to set their hopes on the uncertainty

of riches, but on God, who richly provides us with everything to enjoy. They are to do good, to be rich in good works, to be generous and ready to share, thus storing up for themselves as a good foundation for the future, so that they take hold of that which is truly life.

Wealth can be easy to lose. Even in the past ten to fifteen years we have seen several stock market crashes, and undoubtedly we have more volatility on the way. The truth the apostle Paul shared with Timothy is just as true today as it was 2,000 years ago: If you're putting your hope in wealth, you're storing up treasure in the wrong place.

If you're putting your hope in wealth, you're storing up treasure in the wrong place.

I've witnessed wealth management destroy happiness in numerous ways, and one of them stems from people putting their hope in their investments and retirement accounts. I have seen many clients become enamored with holding on to this wealth, but I have never seen a client lose sleep over holding onto income. For some reason, once individuals see their retirement account value reach a number like $1 million, for instance, it becomes a fixed line. The number can go up, but it certainly can never dip lower than that; otherwise, anxiety sets in.

While working, people get used to the feeling that their wealth is always increasing. They grow accustomed to seeing it increase as they continually save more over the course of a career. However, if you have done your planning

The shark fin will feel more like a bottomless roller coaster than an expected change in financial trajectory.

well, it should actually resemble a shark fin. Picture this fin as first increasing your account value until retirement. Here, you've reached the top of the fin, but once at the top, you begin spending your income down the other side. You have saved it, so now you should spend it. After all, if you don't, your kids certainly will! If you are not going to spend it, you should still have a plan for it, a specific life goal for how you will pass it to the next generation. Even with succession plans, however, if you fall for the trap of placing your self-worth in your net worth, it will be very difficult to see it dwindle. The shark fin will feel more like a bottomless roller coaster than an expected change in financial trajectory.

YOUR PLAN FOR RETIREMENT INCOME

A wealth management plan will protect, preserve, and grow your wealth. This is the typical approach of wealth managers, and it makes sense from a wealth-building perspective. In fact, we have some clients whose goal is just that. As we have illustrated, though, the issue is that it is very difficult to change gears and begin to draw from the wealth you have accumulated. This is why I advocate so strongly for a retirement income plan. From this mindset, you can adequately plan for your daily needs and spending goals. Therefore, you can rely on a consistent "paycheck," rather than a fixed pool of money that gets smaller by the day. A key component in the financial process is developing strategies for retirement income. The goal is to systematically combine the right tools and techniques to create income that will support the lifestyle you envision.

This also plays right into the hands of practicing retirement. After all, decades of work have made us very good at income. We have practiced and are familiar with paychecks. However, most of us are not used to constant withdrawals and burning through our savings accounts. Retirement income allows you to plan well for travel, entertainment, charitable giving, and every other aspect of life, just as you always have. To do this, we have grown adept at moving from assets on a statement to real dollars tied to our clients' life goals.

I love connecting people's money with their passions because this is the gateway to assessing our clients' true wealth statements. In fact, one of the most significant statements a client ever made to me was a woman who had a family history of Alzheimer's disease. She had considerable money saved, and after reviewing her accounts, she looked at me and said, "Ben, I want to spend that money now while I can remember spending it." She wanted to enjoy giving it to her children, donating it to charity, traveling and accumulating rich experiences, and more. So her income plan was very frontloaded because she understood that after a decade, a significant retirement account balance wasn't going to do much for her quality of life. She knew that someday she would be in a state in which she would be losing her mental capacity.

Income is your ability to give and to do, whereas wealth becomes an ever-decreasing mountain to manage. Not only is it difficult to draw from wealth for your own needs, it is also much harder to be generous with it. Tithing and charitable contributions become more painstaking when viewed through the classic wealth-management lens. But with income, the future is sturdy and every dollar has a plan and a purpose. So remember, wealth doesn't buy happiness, but income does.

Income is your ability to give and to do.

CHAPTER NINE

LEGACY

In simplest terms, legacy is what you are going to be remembered for. It is the sum of what you have added to society and the essence of your life that lives on in and through others. Of this, the former president of South Africa, Nelson Mandela, aptly said, "What counts in life is not the mere fact that we have lived. It is what difference we have made in the lives of others that will determine the significance of the life we lead." Your legacy and mine is what we leave that will live on past today and into forever.

In my lifetime, though, what I have learned about legacy is that it is not first about the future. Instead, it is about what I am doing right now. What am I teaching my children, and how am I setting them up to live well and leave a legacy of their own? Our ability to leave a legacy may increase as we grow older, but it doesn't begin at any given age. Someone who leaves a powerful legacy has a life that extends beyond the grave. Yes, this is seen in charitable trusts but also in those who have made deep deposits into the lives of others.

As we age, the importance of our self-worth and positive self-image becomes more important. The end of our life is drawing nearer by the moment, and we can feel it; we can feel the time slipping away. So we look back on our lives and hope to find seeds of meaning planted that are growing into trees of their own. If we have consistently added value to people, what can be better than to reminisce about the positive impact we have had? But even better, if you are reading this book, you can add value to someone's life today. You can foster a greater legacy or begin to live a new one right now.

> **You can foster a greater legacy or begin to live a new one right now.**

I heard John Maxwell speaking about his father, who had recently moved into a retirement home. For many of us, this is the end of life that we dread, but Maxwell's dad is having the time of his life. In fact, his new purpose is to be the unofficial and unpaid welcome committee. He greets newcomers to their community with a smile, a handshake, and an invitation to the card game. The point is that to leave a legacy does not mean only philanthropic contributions. While it may mean that, it can also be the way you influenced your children, who in turn influence your grandchildren. You never know where the ripple ends. Your role is simply to positively contribute to your sphere of influence, no matter how big or small.

A GRAND LEGACY FROM
A SMALL PLATFORM

In Chapter Four, I stated that selfishness and significance cannot coexist and that retirement is selfish if done wrong. So what is the right way? If I have ever seen anyone live it out, it was my Grandpa Ervin. He did not have a large platform; he did not have a larger-than-life personality. He was quiet and soft-spoken. He worked two careers, farming and concrete. He worked as a farmer until he suffered a stroke in his mid-forties. Then my dad stepped in and took over because my grandfather became unable to manage the farm any longer. However, he didn't let the stroke stop him there.

He moved on to a second career working for the Minnesota Department of Transportation in concrete. He was an excellent inspector, very detail oriented and proficient in his work. And though neither farming nor concrete left him a wealthy man by worldly standards, he passed on a rich legacy that he would never be fully aware of. You see, he modeled generosity, giving, and sharing resources more than anyone I have ever seen, and it deeply impacted me. Though he did not have much, he was never selfish with his money.

In fact, he is one of only a few people I have ever seen in my life who gave so much money away that the IRS actually limited what he could deduct on his tax return. The only reason I got to see this is because I did his taxes. Currently, the IRS will not allow anyone to deduct more than 50 percent of their adjusted gross income. You have to carry it forward. My grandpa, by percentage, gave away more of his income than any person I have ever seen.

Now, how far will his legacy of selflessness and generosity go? Because of my grandfather, I make sure that my girls see me giving and that they participate in it. We go to fundraisers, and I want them to understand how important it is to be generous with what God has provided us. I am intentional about showing my children what my grandfather passed down to me. Even if we cannot deduct it, I want them to see me give because tax deductions are not our motivation for giving. This mindset and behavior in my life are not

I am intentional about showing my children what my grandfather passed down to me.

because I am such a great guy. Instead, it is because of my grandfather's legacy. The impact from him to me will be exponential because of the number of lives touched. Though my grandpa stood behind a small podium, he also stood atop a larger platform than he would ever understand.

IMPORTANCE OF LEGACY

My understanding of legacy has also been formative for my company. There are three Ts in our logo that form a tree. Often, people think it is a nice play on my last name, Taatjes. However, the Ts actually represent the time, talent, and treasure entrusted to us all. One of the places this has been most exemplified for me is in the Parable of the Talents in Matthew 25.

One Sunday morning, I sat in church listening to my pastor preach on this text. As he spoke, I began thinking about my clients in this day and age. How amazing it is that such a large segment of our society is even able to think about retirement! And not only do they have monetary provision, but they also have time and a wealth of experience, knowledge, and wisdom. In short, they have time, talent, and treasure.

To synopsize, a wealthy master who was leaving on a journey entrusted three of his servants with his property.

To the first he gave five talents; to the second, two; and to the third, one. Upon his return, he called the servants to him and asked them to recount how they had stewarded the resources he had given them. The first two servants entrusted with five and two talents, respectively, had each doubled their master's investment. To them he said, "Well done, good and faithful servant. You were faithful in little, and I now make you ruler over much." But the third servant approached with less desirable news. Instead of multiplying it, he had hoarded the single talent given to him by burying it in the ground. To this, the master said, "You wicked and slothful servant! Take what you have and give it to the first servant with ten talents. Because to everyone who has, more will be given, but to those who have not, even what they have will be taken away."

Retirees can choose not to work, and that time has been entrusted to them. So when you retire, make certain that you do something with it. How can you use your income like my Grandpa Ervin did? How can you be generous and give it away? And consider your talent. I cannot think of a group with more wisdom to share then people approaching retirement. They have lived full lives and seen incredible changes in our world. Their perspective is so valuable and has such a powerful impact when shared. And just as with the two faithful servants in the parable, the gift is multiplied.

We have each been given something, even if it is in varying amounts. So when I hear people say they have nothing to give, I think that if they would look a little harder, they would find that they do. Whether you are of high or low net worth, you likely have more to give than you realize. You may not know it, but God gave each of us a purpose and a calling, and our task is to discover that calling, not create it.

My Grandpa Ervin modeled hard work, generosity, and how to treat a family. This was passed down to my father, who affirmed it and taught it to me. When I look back to my childhood, these two men loom large. They are the reason I am who I am today, and I strive to continue their legacy. Today, the first lesson on money that my father taught me through my dirt bike colors everything I do in business. He taught me how to respect money, yet understand its limits. How to appreciate it, but never to worship it. Whenever I start holding onto my wealth, I am reminded that I was born into this family that loved me and raised me to be a God-fearing man and to honor Him in all I do, and that is why I am where I am today.

What is your legacy? What is the mark you are leaving on your corner of the world? Is your platform small, like my grandfather's, or large? Remember this: its size does not dictate its impact. The boldest of messages can be declared from the smallest of stages. No matter where you are in life, the way you live today shapes your legacy, which can endure forever. This is true wealth, treasure stored in people whom you love and then to love others in return. You will never know how far your ripple will go, but God certainly does; all He's called you and me to do is to make a splash.

CONCLUSION

FULL CIRCLE

If you have ever traveled to a developing country, you know that motorcycles, or "motos," are a way of life, and Haiti is no exception. I have had the opportunity on five occasions to visit a Haitian orphanage my wife and I support. In my trips to this beautiful but challenged country,[8] I have seen motos carrying everything imaginable. From twenty-two chickens, a quarter of beef, and even a family of seven crammed onto one moto, they are the true workhorses of Haitian transportation. In fact, I've personally ridden with two Haitian men, five twenty-foot pieces of pipe, and miscellaneous tools and parts for a building project we were working on.

---

8. Haiti's people and geography are among the most beautiful I've ever encountered. However, Haiti is also a country ravaged by natural disasters, plagued by economic hardship, and suffering from governmental corruption.

On my fourth trip to Haiti, I decided it wasn't quite enough to simply watch these motos cruising the countryside. My inner child needed to be awakened and recapture the glory of those days driving dirt roads and gravel pits near our old farm. One particularly rainy afternoon, two missionary friends and I took a short dirt bike ride to find a waterfall hidden in the mountains. On our return home, we ran into some flooded streams and attempted to ford them. We navigated through five-foot-deep water for several hundred yards, and thankfully made it through! However, these weren't high-end motorcycles, but small, older, and poorly built machines not designed for such crazy travel. A few miles from home, our travels proved too much for the bike I'd borrowed from my missionary friend. It sputtered to a halt, and I had to be towed back to our village. What a scene for the locals we were: three Americans giggling like kids as our motos limped back to the compound. We went straight to work on the bike and had it working again in a few hours.

At dinner that night, my missionary friend related that this moto was his primary transportation and how much he relied on it. This sparked an hour-long conversation about our mutual love for dirt bikes (which is what got us into trouble in the first place!). We recounted stories, and he shared his dream bike with me. It's always fun to imagine my "what ifs" with someone who appreciates them as much as I do. In all, it was a wonderful way to end an adventurous day.

We soon completed our trip and returned to Minnesota. Once home, the director of the orphanage informed me that a container was to be shipped to the missionaries we had just visited. He asked me if there was anything I would like to send along to them because there was plenty of room. That's when I made a special pilgrimage back to Motor Sports of Willmar, where I had bought my now-infamous dirt bike so many years earlier, and wouldn't you know, the moment I entered I saw my friend's dream bike polished and sparkling on that showroom floor. So I bought it and shipped it to Haiti to replace the one we had nearly drowned in the swollen Haitian rivers. Later, I received a picture of him standing beside his brand-new bike with the biggest smile I have ever seen.

> **I made a special pilgrimage back to Motor Sports of Willmar.**

Now, I certainly do not share that story to draw attention to such a small gift. Instead, I want to pull the curtain back on how God orchestrates both the way and the opportunities we have to be generous. Decades later, I was able to return to the very showroom where my dad had taught me so much about money, stewardship, and hard work and extend his legacy even beyond our country's borders. You see, it is not about me, and it never was, just as it is not about you, and if things go right, it never will be.

Happiness and fulfillment are possible only when we lose ourselves and find joy in adding value to others. Sometimes it's through harrowing rides across rising Haitian streams or in a small-town showroom where a simple purchase brings you full circle and benefits someone else in the process. Whatever it looks like for you, just know that God has already prepared the way and that there can be no greater happiness than walking along that path. Your legacy is being made even as you read these words. So what will you do with the time, talent, and treasure that have been entrusted to you as you approach retirement? Rewrite the American story of retirement, and repurpose your life for further contribution, legacy, and significance.

ABOUT THE AUTHOR

Ben Taatjes is the founder and CEO of Taatjes Financial Group—a leading retirement planning firm with two offices in west-central Minnesota.

Ben opened Taatjes Financial's doors in 2006, and did so with the belief that money alone doesn't make us happy. Since then, he's built a team upon that foundation.

Ben's passion is helping people move their financial assets from numbers on a page into real life. This means assets are converted to match people's "true wealth." From folks on the cusp of retirement to those just getting

BEN TAATJES
Founder and CEO,
Taatjes Financial Group

WEBSITE:
RetireRepurposed.com

OFFICE:
320-222-4236

EMAIL:
ben@taatjesfinancial.com

TWITTER:
@BenTaatjes

started, helping clients achieve their goals is what makes Ben tick. Ultimately, this means building lasting relationships with everyone who walks through his doors.

When he isn't in the office, you can usually find Ben on an outdoor adventure, making memories with his family, or on an annual trip to Haiti to see how the rest of the world lives. Ben lives with his wife, Megan, and daughters, Lauren and Addilyn, in west-central Minnesota.

ABOUT TAATJES FINANCIAL

Taatjes Financial Group is a leading retirement planning firm headquartered in Willmar, MN. Founded in 2006, the company has gone through exponential growth over the past few years after founder and CEO, Ben Taatjes, made a dramatic shift in the business. Prior to the shift, the firm had a focus and goal tied to assets under management, a common practice among financial firms.

WEBSITE:
TaatjesFinancial.com

OFFICE:
320-222-4236

EMAIL:
info@taatjesfinancial.com

FACEBOOK:
facebook.com/taatjesfinancial

ADDRESS:
1104 19th Ave SW
Willmar, MN 56201

But after embracing the Zig Ziglar quote, "You will get all you want in life if you help enough other people get what they want," the firm now has a simple focus of helping others get what they want and tracking number of lives changed.

Coincidentally, after changing the focus/goal the small financial planning company easily blew through the seemingly unattainable asset based goal and has continued to grow at a pace they never imagined.

The firm's mission statement, "We partner with individuals, families, and businesses to change lives and inspire true wealth," is embraced in every aspect of the business. In an effort to meet the needs of their retiring clients, the firm now has a professional counselor on staff who can address the emotional needs of his clients in or near retirement. The innovative work being done at Taatjes Financial Group is what sets them apart and above the competition in a very crowded retirement advice market.

Taatjes Financial Group is not a registered broker/dealer or independent investment advisory firm.